THE

DEBT

CODE

The Ultimate Guide to getting out of Debt and Living a Debt-Free Life

GERALD. P. MORGAN

TABLE OF CONTENT

ABOUT AUTHOR:
Graduated from college at the age of 19.
Made my first million dollar at age 20.
Established over 6 businesses before age 25.
I know I can get you out of debt if you will
do all that is in this book.

I don't play by the rules; life itself isn't fair,
so you shouldn't be fair too.

CHAPTER **ONE:**
INTRODUCTION

Every one of us wants to be debt-free. We are a nation in debt. As of late 2019, the average American $7,354 in credit card debts and over $25,700 in non-mortgage debt, which includes car loans and lots more.

The average student loan balance, in the meantime, has hit over $35,144.

There is a fact that still stands, and that fact is this; more than half the total population of Americans spend more than they earn each month, and that is gotten from research from "Pew Research Study," and they use their credit cards to bridge the gap. So, it is very clear and easy to see how many people are actually struggling with debt – and how many actually choose to bury their heads in the sand instead.

For many people in debt, the problems attached to owing so much money is too much to endure – the reason why so many of them choose to.

Often times, we are being struck by disaster, and we are forced to face and confront our circumstances face to face (head-on).
 When we encounter series of unfortunate circumstances which includes – sudden and unexpected job loss, unexpected house damage repair, a severe health challenge or illness can knock your finance off track that you will barely keep up with your monthly payments. It is usually in these kinds of situations that we finally get to realize how severe our financial conditions are
Other times,
We just become too sick, living a life of paycheck to paycheck, and we make a decision that we want to begin a better life – that's a beautiful decision.
We don't have to face disaster first before we make a decision that we do not want to struggle anymore, and we make a decision to live a simpler life.
For lots of people, getting out of debt is the hardest way and the best and best and only

way to take absolute control of their lives and futures.

Shockingly, the space between understanding your obligation is wild, and really escaping responsibility can be created with challenging work and despair. Regardless of what sort of responsibility you're in, taking care of it can take years — or even decades — to escape obligation.

Luckily, a few techniques exist that can make taking care of obligation quicker — and a mess less demanding. In case you're prepared to escape liability, consider these time tested strategies:

Step by step instructions to Get Out of Debt Faster

Lamentably, the space between understanding your obligation is wild, and really escaping responsibility can be created with intricate work and anguish. Regardless of what sort of commitment you're in, taking care of it can take years — or even decades — to escape obligation.

Luckily, a few procedures exist that can make taking care of obligation quicker — and a mess less demanding. In case you're prepared to escape liability, consider these reliable techniques:

CHAPTER TWO:
PAY MORE THAN THE BASE INSTALLMENT

If you convey the standard charge card equalization of $15,609, pay an average 15% APR, and make the base regularly scheduled installment of $625, it will take you 13.5 years to take care of it.

Furthermore, that is just on the off chance that you don't add to the parity meanwhile, which can be a test individually.

Regardless of whether you're conveying MasterCard obligation, individual credits, or understudy advances, probably the most ideal approaches to pay them down sooner is to make more than the base regularly scheduled installment. Doing so won't just assist you with saving money on enthusiasm for the duration of the life of your advance.

However, it will likewise accelerate the result procedure. To keep away from any cerebral pains, ensure your progress doesn't charge any prepayment punishments before you begin.

If you need a poke right now, you can enroll the assistance of some free on the web and versatile obligation reimbursement instruments, as well, similar to Tally, Unbury. Me, or ReadyForZero, all of which can assist you with diagramming and keep tabs on your development as you pay down equalizations.

CHAPTER THREE: ATTEMPT THE OBLIGATION SNOWBALL STRATEGY

In case you're in the state of mind to pay more than the base regularly scheduled installments on your charge cards and different obligations, consider utilizing the obligation snowball strategy to accelerate the procedure much more and gather speed.

As an initial step, you'll need to list the entirety of the obligations you owe from littlest to most significant. Toss the whole of your overabundance assets at the littlest parity, while making the base installments on the entirety of your more significant credits. When the littlest equalization is paid off, begin putting that additional cash toward the following littlest obligation until you take care of that one, etc.

After some time, your little adjusts ought to vanish individually, opening up more dollars to toss at your more significant obligations and advances. This "snowball impact" permits you to square away littler adjusts first — logging a couple "wins" for the mental impact — while letting you spare the biggest credits for last. Eventually, the objective is snowballing the entirety of your additional dollars toward your obligations until they're crushed — and you're at last commitment-free.

CHAPTER FOUR:
GET A SIDE HUSTLE

Assaulting your obligations with the obligation snowball technique will accelerate the procedure, yet acquiring more cash can intensify your endeavors much further. About everybody has an ability or aptitude they can adapt, regardless of whether it's looking after children, yards, cleaning houses, or turning into a remote helper.

With destinations like TaskRabbit, fiverr.com, and Upwork.com, anybody can discover some approach to acquire additional cash as an afterthought. The key is making use of any extra money you win and utilizing it to take care of advances immediately.

The No. 1 standard of individual money is to spend short of what you win. Should you have the need to excel monetarily, it's critical to set aside cash where you can.

However, if you genuinely need to improve your funds, there's the other side of that condition to consider also – getting more cash. With a side hustle or productive leisure activity, you can give yourself a raise on whether your boss needs to or not.

HERE'S A REALITY NOBODY NEEDS TO DISCUSS:

Learning how to bring in cash can improve your funds in manners that setting aside payment mostly can't. There are just such a large number of approaches to spare.

However, there are a high number of methods to acquire extra cash you can use to settle the debt, put something aside for the future, or really have a fabulous time.

20 Ways to Make Money Online

Because of the miracles of the web, it's totally conceivable to get a consistent side pay from the solace/comfort of your own home. If you need to realize how to bring in cash on the web, think about these conceivable outcomes:

Open an Etsy store.
If you have an innovative ability or expertise – regardless of whether it's making workmanship, sewing garments, or making remembrances – you can open an online store on Etsy.com and sell your products for some quick money. With your own Etsy store, you're absolutely responsible for evaluating and, eventually, the amount you make. See our point by point, groundwork, "How to Make Money on Etsy."

Comprehensive reviews on the web.
Locales like Swagbucks and MyPoints.com pay individuals to give their acumens on items or administrations, test versatile applications, or take advantage in statistical surveying. While the payday for these locales is unassuming, taking part much of the time can assist you with gaining additional cash in a short measure of time.

Get paid to look through the Web.
Zoombucks.com pays you to utilize their online interface to look through the web. To qualify, you should be happy to download

their quest bar and use it for regular Internet use. The main requirement that accompanies this "gig" is that you may be paid in gift vouchers rather than money. If you can parlay those gift vouchers into things you have to purchase in any case – like goods or gas – looking through online can be a rewarding method to invest your free energy.

Assess web search tools.
Web crawler evaluators use usually got to web search tools to search out bugs or mistakes. You may not acquire a great deal, yet you can carry out this responsibility in your extra time and from the solace of your own home. To discover gigs, check destinations like Lionbridge, and Appen Butler Hill.

Start a blog.
If you love composing and are enthusiastic about a particular subject, beginning a blog is an incredible method to dispatch an ease side business with minimal expenditure out-of-pocket. All it takes to start is a space/domain name, few/some essential

online help and assistance, and a brain loaded with lots of thoughts and knowledge to share.

Compose and distribute an eBook. You needn't bother with a conventional distributer and money related sponsorship to distribute your own book any longer. Truth be told, Amazon.com makes it absolutely feasible and easy for you to distribute your own eBook and sell it freely – with no money related venture on your part. What's more, with Amazon Kindle eBook distributing, your book will automatically show up on Kindle stores worldwide within 24-72 hours. Simply get set to advertise it yourself via web-based networking media, your blog, or somewhere else on the off chance that you hope to create deals.

Become an independent essayist or supervisor. If you have an enthusiasm for narrating or a foundation recorded as a hard copy or altering, it's conceivable to discover independent composition or altering work on the web. To look through accessible employment opportunities, look at destinations like UpWork.com and Problogger.net. You can likewise check conventional places of work, for example, Indeed.com and enter "work from home" or "anyplace" in the area field.

Get into associate advertising. In case you're dynamic person via web-based networking media and have a huge following or fanbase, you could parlay those associations into some quick money with an exhaustive partner advertising methodology. By turning into an offshoot advertiser, you'll sell things through your own connections attached to locales like Amazon.com, ClickBank.com, and Commission Junction.

Gain money back for shopping.
Getting money back on your buys is an intelligent decision, and Visa rewards aren't the primary acceptable money-back technique out there. With a site like ShopAtHome, you can win money back on buys made with affirmed shippers. Many continuous customers additionally love the

Ibotta application, which lets you win cashback on each purchase.

Purchase and sell space names. In case you're acceptable at finding famous yet unfamiliar space names, you can make some money as an afterthought by purchasing and exchanging sites.

Consider it an advanced land theory. Areas are accessible on GoDaddy.com for as meager as $2.99 every year, except are in some cases exchanged at far more significant expenses: According to Business Insider, the site MM.com sold for $1.2 million dollars in 2014. When you locate the ideal space name to exchange, you can advertise it on Flippa.com for a level charge.

Bring in cash on YouTube. People who love the feature and have other online hustles should consider making their own YouTube channel. If you're interested — and intriguing — you can use the phase to publicize backup things, sell things you create yourself, or get advancement pay for your easygoing instructional activities or drawing in accounts. At the point when you start the ball rolling, YouTube offers an accessory program that can help you with adjusting your business further.

Become a menial helper.
Menial Modest assistants play out a vast extent of organizations for their clients, which would all be able to be done on the web. Dependent upon the day, they may open and answer to messages, plan online work or blog sections, audit mock letters and recommendations, or perform information entry. You can search for remote helper employments on destinations like UpWork.com and Problogger.net.

Work as an online mediator or interpreter.
On the off chance that you're familiar with an obscure dialect, it looks good to scan for fill in as an online middle person or translator. Dependent upon your individual scope of capacities, you could search for a work disentangling blog passages or eBooks, deciphering recorded activities or

addresses for customers, or deciphering through Skype or another online video administration. Also, on account of the expanded utilization of unknown dialects in the United States, the beginning could genuinely pay off. As indicated by the Bureau of Labor Statistics, work for mediators and interpreters is required to increment 17% all through to 2026.

Oversee web based life for organizations.
If you have got a skill, zeal, or talent for online presence, you might get paid to oversee different stages for other people. Numerous organizations are too bustling running everyday tasks to remain over their Facebook, Twitter, and Pinterest accounts – and will pay somebody with the information and time to do it for them. To secure these positions, ask neighborhood organizations and check destinations like UpWork.com and Problogger.net.

Work remotely for a call place.
Since many call community occupations are area autonomous, looking for some kind of

employment right now a simple method to gain some money from home. Numerous districts list business open doors for call-center agents, including Freelancer.com and SimplyHired.com. Meanwhile, you should check neighborhood work postings for openings and open entryways too.

Lease your vehicle.
In case you're not utilizing your vehicle regularly, you should seriously think about renting it out for some necessary cash. Goals like RelayRides.com and FlightCar.com let you rent your car for a step by step – or even hourly – rate.

Answer questions: In case you're a topic master and well-read, especially in general science, you can get paid for your skill. Destinations like JustAnswer will pay you to respond to questions either on the telephone or on the web. Simply register, enter your subject matter, and begin to start gaining cash as an afterthought.

Lease a room on Airbnb: Living near a voyager domain has its focal points, including the chance of renting a space for an advantage. With home sharing regions like Airbnb, you can rent a room in your home – or even the entire spot – for a day, seven days, or more. In the event that you have additional room and may appreciate the organization of explorers, leasing an apartment is an extraordinary approach to procure some extra money with little effort on your part.

Show English on the web. An industry called VIPKID makes it easier than at any other time to bring in cash instructing English to worldwide youngsters on the internet. You do require a four-year certification and at any rate one year of educating experience to start, yet you can undoubtedly make up to $22 every hour, working only 7.5 hours out of every week.

Become an editor.
A broad scope of associations enrolls capable editors to examine their copy and substance for botches before they disperse. This side hustle is one hustle that could work out for about anybody since you can

telecommute so long as you've got a PC and a web affiliation. You can secure web based editing positions through sites like Indeed.com and FlexJobs.com

CHAPTER FIVE: MAKE (AND LIVE WITH) A NO FRILLS SPENDING PLAN

If you genuinely need to square away obligation quicker, you'll have to cut your costs as much as you can.

Regardless of whether you're attempting to get your obligation leveled out or basically need to develop a secret stash or an upfront installment as fast as could be allowed, a no-frills spending plan is a useful asset to help get you there. It's exactly what it seems like your fundamental costs, and that's it.

A straightforward, stripped-down spending plan can be useful for a forceful reserve funds plan, yet besides, on the off chance that you experience work misfortune, accept a decrease in salary, or need to square away obligation. Regardless of whether you don't have to go stripped down now, no one can really tell when you will. Since my better half and I are independently employed, we plan our spending around an essential, no-frills rendition of our expense that we adjust every month dependent on our fluctuating pay.

Utilizing the lose-lose planning strategy related to a stripped-down spending plan has done some amazing things for both our accounts and our mental soundness. Since regardless of where you are on your way to money related security, it is inconceivably useful to comprehend what your center costs truly signify every month.

Making a Bare-Bones Budget

Be that as it may, you may never realize except if you set aside the effort to make sense of what your no-frills spending plan truly resembles. Need to make a no-frills spending plan of your own? Here's the secret:

Stage 1: Nail down your spending from earlier months.

To make sense of where your cash is going, break out your bank and financial records from the most recent couple of months. Put the entirety of your reasonable costs in like manner sense classes and count them up. Some potential classifications can incorporate things like nourishment, service charges, transportation, garments, eateries, and lease or home loans. Make different ratings varying and make sense of the amount you're spending in each aggregate for the past two months. Make a point to remember obligation reimbursement for its own classification with the goal that you realize precisely the amount you owe every month.

Stage 2: Slash unnecessary costs.

When you've arranged your spending from the past two months, it's an excellent opportunity to perceive what you could live without. Furthermore, that is the place the expression "no-frills" comes into the condition.

Basic costs are things like your home loan or lease installment, utilities, and transportation costs, while unnecessary costs incorporate new outfits for work, suppers at Olive

Garden, and a new home stylistic theme. Fundamentally, anything you could live without is an unimportant cost, so remember that as you make sense of how to get everything down to the stripped-down.

Stage 3: Dig somewhat more profound.

As you trim your spending limit down to the stripped-down, you'll most likely wind up wavering about a portion of your bills. For instance, your link bill is a month to month risk you've become accustomed to; however, do you truly require it? Same thing with your month to month cell phone charge, your amusement spending, and any cash you're spending on unnecessary individual consideration or upkeep.

Keep in mind; a no-frills spending plan should be the manner by which it sounds – stripped down to the fundamentals: asylum, nourishment, and essential everyday costs. In the event that it harms a little to cut so profound, it's simply because it should.

Stage 4: List your new stripped-down costs and count them up.

When you've filtered out the requirements versus needs throughout your life, it's a great opportunity to take another month to month spending plan dependent on your essential, center costs. Everybody's no-frills spending will appear to be unique, yet most will follow a similar general diagram. We as a whole need a spot/niche to live, the utilities turned on, essential transportation, and nourishment in the ice chest, however, everything else is discretionary. Your financial limit ought to mirror that.

When to Break Out Your Bare-Bones Budget

Regardless of whether you're hotly attempting to square away obligation, figuring out how to live on a little level of your salary, or essentially need to spare, however much as could be expected, your stripped-down spending plan can assist you with arriving. Not exclusively would it be able to assist you with recalling which of your costs are needs and needs, however, it can likewise assist you with figuring out how to live – and even flourish – on less cash than you at any point thought conceivable.

Also, you never know, you may even like living on a fundamental rendition of your financial limit without the entirety of the "additional items." The extra cash you spare could go far towards helping you purchase your fantasy house, start a business, or even resign early.

Notwithstanding, the more cash you have spared, the more alternatives you'll have. Also, that is the reason the more significant part of us needs to get our funds together in any case, right? Regardless of anything else, we need decisions.
One instrument you can make and utilize is a no-frills spending plan. With this system, you'll cut your costs as low as they can proceed to live on as meager as workable for whatever length of time that you can.

No-Frills spending will appear to be unique for everybody, except it ought to be without any "additional items" like going out to eat, satellite TV, or pointless spending. While you're living on an exacting spending plan, you ought to have the option to pay impressively more toward your obligations.

Keep in mind. No-frills spending plans are just intended to be impermanent. When you're out of obligation — or significantly closer to your objective — you can begin including discretionary spending once more into your month to month plan.

CHAPTER SIX:
SELL ALL THAT YOU NEEDN'T BOTHER WITH.

In case you're searching for an approach to find some money rapidly this may include the following
Step by step instructions to Get Money Quick: Summed Up

Check out your home.

Take out a loan

Reuse

Pawn or sell things of significant worth

Sell an old PDA

Attempt day work

Sell your plasma

Approach a companion, friend or relative for a credit

Payday credits

Attempt a carport deal

Become a Uber or Lyft Driver

Sell your costly show passes.

Sell your gift vouchers.

Pursue Fiverr

Take a gander at online moneylenders

Open another ledger

Lease a room on Airbnb

Attempt hound strolling or pet sitting.

Find a low maintenance line of work.

On the off chance that you need cash today
or tomorrow.

Attempt the self-evident: Look around your home.

We have to get this off the beaten path first; furthermore, perhaps you haven't thought of this since you're in finished frenzy mode. Check the couch pads, your jeans pockets, old covers in the storeroom, and your vehicle, where extra change may have fallen between the seats. In the event that you haven't stripped your home recently and cleaned yourself out, there must be some cash lying around.

Alright, so you've attempted that. Next, you may move onto.

Take out a loan.

Your charge card may offer the choice of a loan, which permits you to take out money (from an ATM) against your card's credit limit.

The drawback here is that you'll shell out some serious cash for this benefit: Between loan expenses and higher-than-normal premium charges that start accumulating the subsequent you put your hands on the cash, you can without much of a stretch wind up paying $1,000 to get to $800, for instance. All things considered, it's a method to transform your available credit into money. It may pay to check out your possessions first.

Reuse.

In the ten expresses that have bottle store laws, including New York and California, you can return most aluminum and glass containers and jars for five pennies each (10 pennies in Michigan).

They don't need to be your containers: Plenty of individuals are excessively occupied or lethargic to try restoring a six-pack worth of brew or soft drink jars for 30 pennies and basically forget about them for curbside pickup. It may not be garbage day in your neighborhood. However, it definitely is someplace. Top off a 50-gallon waste pack with push-off jars, and you can reclaim them for about $12 – it's only a beginning, yet you can do it over and over, and everything necessary is time and hustle.

If you don't live in a container store state, you can, in any case, money in on recyclables by selling scrap metal. You might not have enough pop or brew jars lying around to make this advantageous — and steel costs are so low at the present time, it's not so much worth the try to go gathering them. In any case, if you do have a great deal of aluminum jars available, or on the off chance that you have any piece metal with copper in it, locate a neighborhood reusing focus and see what you'll get (costs differ uncontrollably by advertise). All things considered, except if you have a great deal of copper pipes lying around the carport, or packs and sacks and sacks of old soft drink jars, everything being equal, we're most likely looking at getting $5 to $20 back.

Pawn or sell things of significant worth.

Consider this one for a little while before you attempt it. On the off chance that you have something extremely important or significant, similar to your father's 1950s model train assortment, your grandma's gold jewelry, or the mint piece assortment that you worked over as a child, selling it might assist put with trip a fire today — yet you truly may end up kicking yourself not far off.

Also, you're probably not going to bring as high a cost for something of significant worth when you're feeling the squeeze to sell it locally and immediately. In any case, contingent upon the seriousness of your circumstance, in the event that you have something important to sell, this might be an ideal opportunity to use it.

A superior choice is burrowing through your storerooms, storage room, and storm cellar for stuff that may even now have some worth, only not to you: An old DVD assortment, your 10-year-old's infant garments or little child trike, or the cappuccino machine (or bread creator, or juicer) that you just utilized once.

In case you're not utilizing the stuff, you most likely needn't bother with it any longer, and you can bear to sell it at a cut-rate cost on the off chance that you need money speedy. Post a free promotion on Craigslist or a neighborhood Facebook Yard Sale gathering and demonstrate that you're willing to convey the things for an expedient exchange.

Sell an old mobile phone.

If you have an old cell phone and you need cash today, look at ecoATM. Type in your ZIP code, and with any karma, you'll see one of their ATMs in your general vicinity. On the off chance that you do, you basically discover the booth and spot the old mobile phone in the ecoATM's test station, where the machine will inspect your telephone — taking note of the model number and condition, among different highlights. It at that point consequently filters the resale showcase for comparable phones and offers you a cost dependent on its worth — in the event that you consent to the value, you'll get the cash on the spot (henceforth the ATM in the name). They additionally acknowledge MP3 players and tablets.

You can likewise sell your old mobile phone for more cash on eBay or Craigslist, the last of which can conceivably yield an equivalent day money deal. In the event that you can hold up somewhat more, a hardware resale site like Gazelle or Flipsy may purchase your old telephone — in any case, since they expect you to deliver the thing, it commonly takes seven days to get paid.

Attempt day work.

Peradventure you don't as of now have an occupation, you can attempt your karma with a day work office in your general vicinity, for example, Labor Works or People Ready. By and large, these employments are of the low-aptitude, low-pay assortment — development aide, mover, retail or stockroom work. Show up before the expected time in the first part of the day, and in case you're picked for an occupation, you'll work that equivalent day and get installment toward the finish of your day of work.

Some time or another worker can secure money positions on Craigslist or by congregating in notable gathering spots like a Home Depot parking area, yet be careful that you're putting yourself in danger of getting scammed or harmed without protection.

Sell your plasma.

In the event that there's a plasma gift focus in your general vicinity, you may have the option to make somewhere in the range of $25 to $50, and chances are, you'll get paid today. Call ahead and ask, obviously, however nowadays, numerous gift places are giving cash cards (like a plastic). By and large, it takes around 30 minutes to give your plasma, yet a first visit may take longer — as long as two hours — since you'll be rounding out administrative work and taking a physical. And keeping in mind that it is anything but a huge amount of cash, numerous contributors can sell plasma two times per week.

And keeping in mind that you've most likely known about selling sperm or eggs, don't get your expectations up: Yes, the youthful and the solid can at times win great cash as sperm or egg benefactors, however, such open doors require broad screenings and long haul responsibilities. Giving blood (sans plasma), then, is an incredible and benevolent activity, yet you, for the most part, won't get cash for it.

Approach a companion, friend, or relative for a credit.

We won't invest a lot of energy in this since it's not as though you should be advised how to move toward a relative or a companion for a credit. Simply realize that it won't be beautiful.

It might be a discussion with a great deal of uncomfortable silence. It might be mortifying. You might be told no. It might be your solitary alternative. Obviously, if your companion or family isn't close by, where they can hand you money, and they wind up sending you cash by means of an application, remember that you will be unable to get some money from them today. Payday credit stores are an alternative (just not a decent one).

I'm not embracing them. No one on this site would. On an annualized premise, financing costs on payday advances convey an average APR of over 300%. In any case, then again, it's an authentic method to get money, and it's superior to ransacking a bank.

On the off chance that you need cash today, you don't have Mastercards to go to, and set off to a relative is out, you could go to a payday advance store in your neighborhood and request an advance. You, for the most part, will require evidence of business (pay stubs) and distinguishing proof; call ahead and ask what they require. You'll most likely need references. Furthermore, you should be certain beyond a shadow of a doubt you can take care of the advance under the predefined terms.

On the off chance that you can't take care of the advance and its heavy enthusiasm inside about fourteen days, by and large, that is the point at which you run into inconvenience. If it's not too much trouble, question yourself, "If things are awful presently, will they truly be better in about fourteen days? Would I be able to repay this credit and the enthusiasm without making more issues?"

I've utilized payday advance stores previously. Thus I realize one does what one needs to do — yet I'm wincing at proposing anybody take out a payday credit. Truly, in light of my own encounters and meetings, I've finished with individuals who have utilized them, I feel like whatever issues you have, you're presumably happier letting them occurring and keeping away from this way. Taking out a payday credit is similar to tolerating a parachute with a gap in it. You may land securely. Yet, would you truly like to face that challenge?

In the event that you need cash inside seven days.

Attempt a carport deal.

See, I know it's not constantly sensible to pull these off; I, for one, wouldn't try attempting. Yet, in the event that you have a tremendous amount of stuff lying around — not by and large garbage, however things you needn't bother with, similar to the previously mentioned DVDs and child's garments — it merits an attempt. Publicize on Craigslist and set up signs in your neighborhood, at that point come Saturday to pull a table out to your carport (accepting you have a garage), load it up with stuff available to be purchased, and take whatever you can get.

Become an Uber or Lyft driver.

This is another choice that may not be reasonable for many individuals. I'm almost sure I'd state, "Forget about it," myself. Then again, on the off chance that you have some personal time, a dependable vehicle, great protection, and not too bad social abilities, you can surely procure some legitimate cash driving individuals around.

The average Uber driver is said to make about $19 to $21 an hour after tolls and some different costs are figured in — in spite of the fact that I've seen different numbers recommending it's nearer to $16, and with Lyft, the normal is said to be less (closer to $11). However, on the in addition to side, you can, for the most part, get your cash in a split second, which wasn't generally the situation with these ride-sharing organizations.

To bring in genuine cash, you'll need to drive around a nice sum and during top hours, for example, Saturday evenings. Likewise, remember the expense of gas and the extra mileage on your vehicle.

Goodness, and for what reason am I saying that it'll take seven days to get paid in case you've paid in a flash? It'll take at any rate that long – and potentially as long as about fourteen days – to pass the underlying individual verification.

Sell those costly show passes.

Kid, I prefer not to recommend this on the off chance that you were truly amped up for going to an up and coming show, game, or a Broadway play. In any case, if you have passes to a major occasion, selling them could be a useful and brisk approach to recover your money related picture on track.

StubHub is most likely the most popular ticket resale site, however different locales have gotten in on the game, as well, including VividSeats and even Ticketmaster. Contingent upon what sort of tickets you have, you could bring in your cashback — to say the least — yet you'll as a rule need to hold up, in any event, a couple of days for the money.

Utilizing StubHub, for instance, after you list your tickets (calculating in their expenses), you'll need to trust that somebody will get them. This can happen rapidly if it's a significant name show or Broadway play, however perhaps one moment if it's a perusing of Elizabethan verse; obviously, setting a low cost will by and large assist them with selling quicker.

When the purchaser gets their tickets — in the event that you transferred PDF e-tickets, they'll get them promptly, and else you'll need to mail them to the purchaser — StubHub starts handling the installment. In case you're paid through PayPal, it'll take as long as five days (a check via the post office will take as long as about fourteen days).

Sell your gift vouchers.

In the event that you have gift vouchers lying around that you never figure out how to utilize – possibly you have $50 to Longhorn Steakhouse. However, you're a vegan – you can sell them at a markdown through gift voucher trade destinations, for example, CardCash.com. When the site gets and checks the equalization on the card (ecards are clearly helpful, yet they'll pay for you to mail in physical gift vouchers), you can get paid in as meager as two days.

Note that you're successfully paying a charge of 15% or a more significant amount of the card's worth, however in case you're really stuck a spot or can't envision utilizing or re-gifting a gift voucher, that might be a little cost to pay for fast cash.

Pursue Fiverr.

In case you're prepared in an attractive aptitude — like realistic or website architecture, SEO composing, or video liveliness — to where you can blast out the work in your rest, you can make a truly fast buck with it on Fiverr. Regardless of whether it's the best long haul procedure for your independent vocation is begging to be proven wrong – and it's one of the least worthwhile gig economy sides hustles out there – however that is not the point; the fact of the matter is that there's the potential for procuring cash rapidly.

You can energize to $995 for help, however numerous if not most gigs despite everything start at only $5 (of which you make $4), so the way to bringing in cash on Fiverr is either working in volume or offering extra custom administrations. Be that as it may, it's free, simple, and speedy to begin, and installment happens decently fast, so in case you're ready to prepare a logo or business card plan absents a lot of exertion, it is anything but a terrible method to take advantage of your innovative abilities.

Take a gander at online loan specialists.

There is an assortment of online banks out there, and if your credit is genuinely acceptable, you can apply for a personal advance on the web and be affirmed right away. The cash will, at present, take a couple of days or even seven days to hit your record, and the financing cost will be higher than, state, a home value advance. Yet, an individual advance from a legitimate organization — and be cautious, for some online moncylcnders are minimal more than payday advance shops on the web — beats

Visa obligation for two or three reasons: Installment advances are preferred for your credit over rotating charge card adjusts, and even a 10% loan cost is desirable over what you'd pay for a loan.
In the event that you need cash inside a month...

Open up another financial balance.

This may seem like a moronic thought, to be perfectly honest, yet a lot of banks nowadays are offering $200 to $300 information exchange rewards to clients who open up another financial record. The catch, however, is that you by and large need to truly open these records. You should be happy to set up an immediate store and put cash in the record, and you regularly don't get the reward for at any rate a month, once in a while, much more. Then again, in the event that you were considering setting off to another bank, at any rate, it's a simple method to make some additional money.

Lease a room on Airbnb.

As you likely know, Airbnb is a well-known site where individuals can lease a room or loft from customary people and sidestep a lodging. In this way, in case you're alright with outsiders, and you live in genuinely all-around visited place — an enormous city, school town, or vacationer zone, for instance — you could bring in some cash leasing a room in your home while you're there, or leasing the whole spot while you're gone. You can hope to make not precisely whatever close by lodgings charge, yet that can at present top $100 every night pretty effectively. Truth be told, Airbnb is the most rewarding of all the sharing economy gigs, as per one examination.

Honestly, be that as it may, this may not be reasonable for many individuals. I wouldn't depend on this in case you're attempting to make your lease, and you're tying up of your resources in one place. In the first place, somebody needs to take a gander at your area and posting photographs and state, "Sure, I'd prefer to remain there," and that might possibly occur inside a month. It might never occur.

Be that as it may, if all works out in a good way, you could have someone leasing your extra room one weekend from now or even tomorrow evening. Furthermore, 24 hours after they check-in, you'll get paid via Airbnb (less a couple of expenses) inside a day in the event that you use PayPal, and in around three days on the off chance that you go with the direct store.

Attempt hound strolling or pet sitting.

On the off chance that you have experience thinking about creatures, you can join as a pet sitter or pooch walker on Rover.com. The organization surveys each new profile independently, which can take as long as five days — and not every person qualifies (past involvement in pets is a major in addition to).

When endorsed, you can get enlisted to walk hounds in your neighborhood or to have them in your home medium-term for upwards of $20 to $40 per night while their

proprietors are away. Connection up your
PayPal account early, and you'll get your
assets three to six days after help is finished,
which means you could be acquiring cash in
under about fourteen days.

Find a low maintenance line of work.

On the off chance that you get a side activity
at some drive-thru eatery or retail chain and
start today, it'll presumably be as long as a
month prior to you get your first check. You
work for two weeks, and after two weeks,
the check comes in. Possibly you'd get paid
sooner — yet as far as I can tell when I've
required money rapidly, it's smarter to be
cynical and plan for the most noticeably
terrible and trust in the best.

 The greater part of us has stuff lying around
that we seldom use and could live without in
the event that we truly expected to. Why not
sell your additional stuff and utilize the
assets to settle your obligations?

On the off chance that you live in a local
that grants it, a classic carport deal is

regularly the least expensive and most straightforward approach to dump your undesirable possessions for a benefit. Else, you can consider selling your things through a transfer shop, one of the numerous online affiliates out there, or a Facebook yard deal gathering.

Get an occasional, low maintenance work.

With the special seasons coming up, nearby retailers are vigilant for adaptable, occasional laborers who can keep their stores operational during the busy, bubbly season. In case you're willing and capable, you could get one of these low maintenance occupations and gain some additional money to use toward your obligations.

Indeed, even outside of the individual seasons, a lot of occasional employments might be accessible. Springtime brings the requirement for occasional nursery laborers and homestead occupations, while summer calls for visit administrators and a wide range of open-air, impermanent specialists from lifeguards to greens keepers. Fall brings regular work for frequented house attractions, pumpkin fixes, and fall gather.

The primary concern: No issue what season it is, a transitory activity without an extended haul responsibility could be inside reached.

Request lower loan costs on your Visas — and arrange different bills.

On the off chance that your charge card financing costs are so high, it feels practically difficult to make progress on your parities, and it merits calling your card guarantor to arrange. In all honesty, requesting lower loan costs is very ordinary. What's more, IF you have a strong history of taking care of your tabs on schedule, there's a decent chance of getting a lower financing cost.

Past Mastercard premium, a few different sorts of bills can, as a rule, be brought down or wiped out too — I featured them in Six

Bills You Can Negotiate Down to Save Money below.

If you have an affection detest relationship with your month to month charges, you're not the only one. While the majority of us appreciate a cutting edge way of life and all the advantages that accompany it, that doesn't mean we really appreciate paying for it.

Be that as it may, did you realize specific month to month bills can be brought down to a lower rate? While a few bills like home loan installments, property duties, and vehicle installments are unchangeable, others can be diminished in case you're willing and ready to wrangle.

Six Bills Worth Negotiating

If you need to bring down your month to month charges no matter how you look at it, it assists with realizing which bills may have some squirm room. This rundown incorporates a portion of the bills that may be most straightforward to limit:

Link or Satellite TV

With such an enormous amount of rivalry right now, and satellite TV suppliers are ordinarily anxious to arrange. As a rule, they understand that it is simpler (and less expensive) to keep the clients they have versus attempting to get another one. Link and satellite suppliers might be greedy, yet they're keen, as well.

If you need to bring your link bill down, call your link organization. Have a rundown prepared with their rival's costs for comparative administrations, and be prepared to express your case. On the off chance that you benefit it enough, you may even be moved to the client maintenance line, where they are prepared to haggle with you.

Also, recall, you, as a rule, can leave if you locate a less expensive rate somewhere else (except if you consented to a two-year arrangement, as DirecTV regularly powers its clients to do).

Network access

Much the same as satellite TV, home Internet administration is exceptionally serious. In the event that your Internet administration is connected to your link supplier, you may have the option to arrange both all at once. In any case, if your Internet is offered through an alternate supplier, a different call might be all together.

In any case, call up your supplier with a rundown of contenders' rates close by — or hit them up in an online visit (if their site has it). At the point when you find a workable pace individual, request that they bring down your bill so as to meet their opposition's early on estimating. Furthermore, recall, the most noticeably awful they can say is no.

Doctor's visit expenses

Regardless of whether you have the cash to take care of your medicinal tabs in full, it bodes well to bring them down on the off chance that you can. Destitute emergency clinics are regularly ready to take not precisely the charged sum in case you're willing to come up with all required funds and early. (Significant safety net providers arrange limited rates regularly.) At the least, you ought to inquire.

At the point when I had both of my little girls at my neighborhood emergency clinic, for instance, I confronted a $4,000 out-of-pocket max. When I got the entirety of my emergency clinic charges, I arranged a 30% rebate for covering via telephone and that day. In this way, rather than paying $4,000, I paid $2,800! All it took was a 20-minute call to spare an incredible $1,200.

Charge card Interest Rates

In case you're discontent with your charge card's financing cost, you should seriously mull over looking for another card. In any case, you will not have to switch cards totally. Just by calling your card backer and asking, you may verify a lower rate on the card you have.

In the event that you have a past filled with capable credit use, point to it as verification that you merit a credit extension with better terms. Furthermore, be happy to walk; on the off chance that you let them realize you are eager to move your adjust or get a contender's card rather, they will be increasingly disposed to give in to your solicitation.

Vehicle Insurance Rates

Vehicle protection is another profoundly severe industry. Hence, you regularly can arrange genuine limits and investment funds — and with next to no exertion on your part. At times, insurance agencies may much offer an "off the top" rebate to keep you as a client.

Different ways you can spare incorporate pursuing web-based charging (rather than paper explanations), packaging your mortgage holders or leaseholders protection with a similar guarantor, or pursuing a sheltered driver program, for example,

Allstate Drivewise. You can likewise survey your present inclusion and cut back on unnecessary things you needn't bother with, similar to rental vehicle substitution on the off chance that you have a reinforcement vehicle, or emergency aides on the off chance that you as of now have AAA.

To discover what your choices are, call your insurance agency, and reveal to them you're searching for approaches to save money on your regularly scheduled installments. On the off chance that they need to keep you as a client, they'll be transparent about your choices.

Month to month Rent Payments

On the off chance that you think lease costs are constantly unchangeable, reconsider. Perfect and reliable leaseholders with a protracted history have a decent possibility at arranging their lease — and that is particularly valid in the event that they intend to remain as long as possible.

At the point when your rent is up, approach your landowner for the ideal arrangement. If you intend to remain sometime, you can considerably offer to sign a more drawn out term rent to mirror that dedication. In any case, you'll be in the best situation to score a rebate in the event that you have been a decent leaseholder from the earliest starting point. At the point when you're dependable and reliable, it's less expensive for a landowner to keep you as a leaseholder — even with a markdown — at that point, it is for them to supplant you.

It Never Hurts to Ask

With regards to bringing your bills down, recollect that it never damages to inquire. The most noticeably awful any of your suppliers can say is no, yet an ideal situation could prompt huge, progressing investment funds. In any case, you'll never comprehend what may occur on the off chance that you never get the telephone.

Continuously recollect, the most exceedingly awful anybody can say is no.

What's more, the less you pay for your fixed costs, the more cash you can toss at your obligations.

In case you're not the arranging type, assistance like TrueBill can help. The application will audit your buy history to discover overlooked memberships and other rehashing charges you should cut from your financial limit, and it can even bring a few bills down for you.

Consider an equalization move.

In the event that your charge card organization won't move on financing costs, it might merit investigating a parity move. With some equalization move offers, you can verify 0% introduction APR for as long as a year and a half, in spite of the fact that you may need to pay a parity move expense for the benefit.

On the off chance that you have a charge card balance, you could attainably pay off during that time allotment, moving the equalization to a card like the Discover it®

Balance Transfer could set aside your cash on the premium while at the same time helping you pay down obligation quicker.

Use 'discovered cash' to take care of equalizations.

A great many people go over some sort of "discovered cash" consistently. Perhaps you get a yearly raise, a legacy, or reward grinding away. Or on the other hand, possibly, you rely on a major fat expense discount each spring. Whatever kind of "discovered cash" it will be, it could go far toward helping you become obligation-free.

Each opportunity you go over any strange wellsprings of salary, you can utilize those dollars to take care of a significant piece of obligation. In case you're doing the obligation snowball technique, utilize the cash to square away your littlest equalization. Also, in case you're left with just large adjusts, you can utilize those dollars to remove an enormous lump from anything that's left.

Drop costly propensities.

In case you're paying off debtors and reliably missing the mark every month, assessing your propensities may be the best thought at this point. Regardless, it bodes well to take a gander at the little ways you're going through cash day by day. That way, you can assess whether those buys are justified, despite all the trouble — and think of approaches to limit them or dispose of them.

On the off chance that your costly propensity is smoking or drinking, that is a simple one — quit. Liquor and tobacco fail to help you with the exception of remain among you and your long haul objectives. On the off chance that your costly propensity is somewhat less flammable – like a day by day latte, eatery snacks during work hours, or cheap food — the best arrangement of assault is typically chopping path down with the objective of taking out these practices or supplanting them with something more affordable.

Step away from the _____.

We're totally enticed by something. For some, it may be the nearby shopping center or our preferred online store. For other people, it may be driving by a most loved eatery and wishing we could fly inside for a most loved feast. Also, for those with an inclination for spending, having a Mastercard in their wallet is an excessive amount of compulsion to hold up under.

Whatever your greatest enticement is, it's ideal to keep away from it through and through when you're settling obligation. At the point when you're continually enticed to spend, it very well may be hard to dodge new obligations, not to mention take care of old ones.

Thus, dodge allurement any place you can, regardless of whether that implies taking an alternate way home, maintaining a strategic distance from the Internet, or keeping the refrigerator supplied, so you aren't enticed to spend too much. What's more, If you should, stash those charge cards away in a sock cabinet for now. You can continually bring them to pull out once you're without obligation.